ROADMAP

The Law Student's Guide to Meaningful Employment

THIRD EDITION

NEIL W. HAMILTON

Cover design by Elmarie Jara/ABA Design

Printed in the United States of America.

27 26 25 24 23   5 4 3 2 1

A catalog record for this book is available from the Library of Congress.

Discounts are available for books ordered in bulk. Special consideration is given to state bars, CLE programs, and other bar-related organizations. Inquire at Book Publishing, ABA Publishing, American Bar Association, 321 N. Clark Street, Chicago, Illinois 60654-7598.

www.shopABA.org

To my wife, Uve, whose love and support inspire me each day to be as kind and selfless as she is.

CONTENTS

ACKNOWLEDGMENTS

This third edition of the Roadmap is a complete revision of the second edition. Since the first edition was published in 2015, and the second edition in 2018, we have continued to learn how more effectively to go where the students are developmentally to help them achieve their goals of bar passage and meaningful post-graduation employment. I am deeply grateful for all the student suggestions over the years that led to this much shorter third edition of the Roadmap.

I want to give particular thanks to those who read earlier drafts of this edition and gave me editing suggestions: my University of St. Thomas School of Law colleagues Jerry Organ and David Grenardo; my students David Cheney, Jack Golbranson, Robert Rohloff, Sean Smallwood, and Emma Theis; and my Santa Clara Law School colleague Theodora Pina. Brady King provided much-needed help on the figures. Most importantly, I want to express my deepest gratitude to my wife, Uve, who helped by reading and commenting on many drafts and who has been tirelessly supportive over so many years in this project of helping the students connect the dots to be successful in becoming lawyers and serving others in meaningful employment.

CHAPTER 1

INTRODUCTION TO THE ROADMAP STEPS

Do you hope to find post-graduation employment that fits your passion, interests, and strengths? If meaningful employment with the potential for career advancement is your goal, this book is your roadmap to develop and implement a written professional development plan to achieve your goal.

To reach your goal, you need to understand your passion and motivating interests with respect to your work, your current strengths, and your future development with respect to all of the capacities and skills that employers and clients want. You must take ownership to build on your existing strengths and skills while learning how to communicate to employers (and eventually clients) how those strengths and skills will bring value to their team. Ultimately, this comes in the form of a **persuasive story** when answering the question "Why should we hire you?" Envision the development of your most persuasive story essentially as lawyering for yourself to influence a target audience of your most promising employers.

When you have little or no experience in the actual practice of law, you have a major challenge to discern your passion and motivating interests and your strengths in the context of the capacities and skills legal employers and clients want. In general, the required curriculum in your three years of law school is not structured to help you address this challenge.

A brief explanation of how medical education helps medical students address this challenge will demonstrate why you must take proactive ownership of your professional development to reach your goals. The first 18 to 24 months of medical school are focused on the basic doctrinal knowledge and analytical skills a physician needs.[1] Your first year of law school is very similar with respect to the basic knowledge and analytical skills a lawyer needs.[2]

The third and fourth years of medical school require approximately 80 weeks of rotations (usually 6 to 7 required and some elective) at hospitals and clinics in a number of specialties where the student interacts with patients, resident physicians, nurses, and other staff who see the student's work and give feedback and assessment. These rotations give students a breadth of experience to thoughtfully discern their passions, motivating interests, and strengths that best fit with a practice area and type of patient the student wants to serve. The student's reflection on the experiences, feedback, and assessment in the rotations makes clearer the student's path into a residency program and how to improve the student's skills.[3]

The *key* point for you to understand is that, in contrast to medical education, the required curriculum in your 2L and 3L years in law school is not formally structured to provide you with a breadth of experiences so that you can thoughtfully discern your passion, motivating interests, and strengths that best fit a practice area, the type of client you want to serve, and the type of employing organization you want to join. Even if you entered law school with enough experience so that you know your best fit with respect to your area of practice, type of client, and type of employing organization, the required curriculum in the 2L and 3L years is not structured to develop the full array of capacities and skills needed for your success in practice. *You must take ownership to create and implement a professional development plan to reach these goals.*

---

[1] At the end of the second year, a medical student usually takes Step 1 of the United States Medical Licensing Examination to assess whether the student understands and can apply important concepts of the sciences basic to the practice of medicine.

[2] The pre-clinical period of medical school usually also includes the basics of interviewing and examining a patient, which is not generally true in the first year of legal education with respect to a client.

[3] A medical student usually takes Step 2 of the United States Medical Licensing Examination at the end of the third year or in the fourth year. Step 2 assesses the student's medical knowledge and basic patient-centered skills for the provision of patient care under supervision.

For the summer between your 1L and 2L years, your 2L year, the summer between your 2L and 3L years, and your 3L year, you are in charge of choosing "rotation" experiences inside and outside of the law school where you interact with lawyers (including professors), staff, and clients to obtain the experiences you need to discern your best fit for meaningful post-graduation employment. At the same time, you should be seeking feedback and assessment of your work and developing your capacities and skills beyond the basic doctrinal knowledge and analytical skills needed for career success. You also should be developing good evidence employers will value that indicates you are at a later stage of development on these important non-technical capacities and skills.

How to decide which "rotation" experiences you should be proactively seeking during your remaining time in law school? Figure 1 provides a visual outline highlighting the discernment questions about meaningful employment you want your rotational experiences to help you decide.

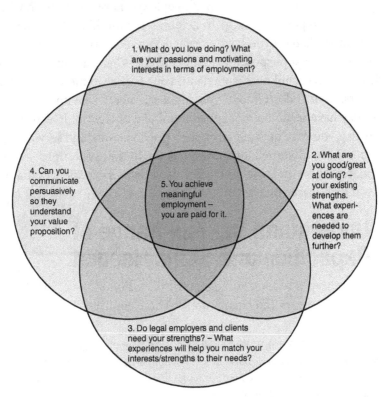

Figure 1 Getting Experiences to Help Answer Your Discernment Questions about Meaningful Employment

The ten steps in this Roadmap process will help your discernment to answer the questions in Figure 1. The process will lead to meaningful post-graduation employment and a career-long strength of professional development planning.

Following is a summary of the ten steps. The Roadmap online template in Chapter 2 that you access after you have read Chapter 1 asks you to fill in answers on each step and then to discuss your professional development plan with a coach.

1. Assess Your Passion and Motivating Interests

The first step is to assess your passion and motivating interests from your previous work and service experiences. What are the characteristics of past work/service where you have found the most meaning and positive energy? Is there a particular group of people you have served from whom you have drawn positive energy in helping? Try thinking about the best, most memorable days you have ever had in your work or service—days when you felt most purposeful and energized. What was happening that made these days stand out? Note that if your answer to these questions is some version of "I don't know," you could ask others who know you well when they have seen you most purposeful and energized. It also may be simply that you have not yet had enough previous work and service experiences to have discerned a tentative answer to these questions, and the Roadmap process leads you to try a wide variety of experiences that will help you with discernment.

2. Understand the Full Range of Capacities and Skills Needed

The second step is to look at the empirical studies on the capacities and skills legal employers and clients want.[4] These empirical studies support

---

[4] Appendix A (pp. 17–27) in a 2022 book by Neil W. Hamilton and Louis D. Bilionis, *Law Student Professional Development and Formation: Bridging Law School, Student, and Employer Goals*, summarizes 15 empirical studies that define the foundational competencies that legal employers and clients want.

the conclusion that the following six traditional technical competencies in Table 1 that law schools emphasize are necessary but not sufficient to meet client and legal employer needs in changing markets.

Table 1 Traditional Technical Capacities and Skills That Law Schools Emphasize and Clients and Legal Employers Want

---

1. Knowledge of doctrinal law in the basic subject areas

2. Legal analysis

3. Legal research

4. Written and oral communication in the legal context

5. Legal problem-solving[5]

6. Knowledge of the law-of-lawyering responsibilities to clients and the legal system[6]

The additional capacities and skills that empirical studies indicate that clients and legal employers need from students and lawyers in changing markets are set forth in Table 2.

---

[5] While your 1L courses give you some understanding of knowledge of doctrinal law in the basic subject areas, legal analysis, legal research, and written and oral communication in the legal context, legal problem-solving/legal judgment are more challenging to define. The focus here is on how legal employers define legal problem-solving. An empirical study of five large firm competency models points toward four major elements for good legal problem-solving: (1) recognition of risks and evaluation of alternative courses of action with a recommendation on the most reasonable course of action; (2) creativity and strategic thinking; (3) understanding the client's best interests in the larger context of the client's situation and business; and (4) dialogue with other lawyers to get feedback and greater insight. Legal problem-solving develops with experience and reflection on experience. *See* NEIL HAMILTON, ROADMAP: THE LAW STUDENT'S GUIDE TO MEANINGFUL EMPLOYMENT 113–14 (2d ed. 2018).

[6] The sixth capacity/skill, regarding knowledge of the law-of-lawyering responsibilities, is covered in the required Professional Responsibility course. These six competencies are listed in STANDARDS AND RULES OF PROCEDURE FOR APPROVAL OF LAW SCHOOLS 2022–2023 Standard 302 (a)–(c) (AM. BAR ASS'N), https://www.americanbar.org/content/dam/aba/administrative/legal_education_and_admissions_to_the_bar/standards/2022-2023/2022-2023-standards-and-rules-of-procedure.pdf.

Table 2 The Additional Capacities and Skills That Clients and Legal Employers Want

1. Superior client focus and responsiveness to the client
2. Exceptional understanding of the client's context and business
3. Effective communication skills, including listening and knowing your audience
4. Creative problem-solving and good professional judgment in applying all of the previously noted competencies
5. Ownership over continuous professional development (taking initiative) of both the traditional technical competencies in Table 1 and the additional capacities and skills in this table
6. Teamwork and collaboration
7. Strong work ethic
8. Conscientiousness and attention to detail
9. Grit and resilience
10. Organization and management of legal work (project management)
11. An entrepreneurial mindset to serve clients more effectively and efficiently in changing markets (this includes understanding technology to reduce costs)

Note that the National Conference of Bar Examiners, based on its empirical studies of the capacities and skills that newly licensed lawyers need, has proposed a modification of the Uniform Bar Exam called the Next Generation Bar Exam. Many states are considering these proposals. In addition to the capacities and skills in Table 1, the bar examination would include the skills of client advising and counseling, client relationships and management, negotiation and dispute resolution, and investigation and evaluation.[7]

Figure 2, building on the Thomson Reuters Delta Model approach,[8] visually represents a Foundational Competencies Model that captures

---

[7] Nat'l Ass'n of Bar Examiners, *Final Report of the Testing Task Force* (Apr. 2021), https://nextgenbarexam.ncbex.org/wp-content/uploads/TTF-Final-Report-April-2021.pdf.

[8] In a white paper, Thomson Reuters presented what it has titled the "Delta" model of lawyer competency. The model groups lawyer competencies into three categories, with each category represented by one of the three sides of a triangular figure. The base of the triangle represents the technical skills traditionally associated with lawyering. The upper two sides of the triangle represent "personal effectiveness" factors and "business and operations" competencies, respectively. *See* Natalie Runyon & Alyson Carrel, *Adapting for*

and conceptually organizes all these major competencies[9] that clients and legal employers need.

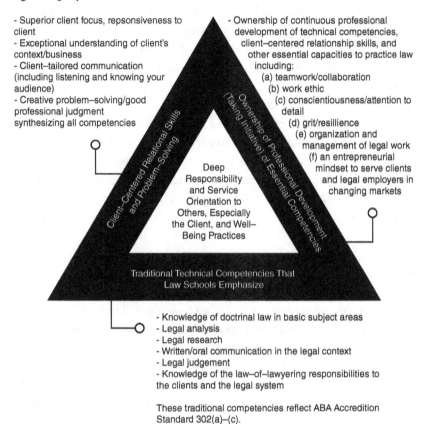

Figure 2 Foundational Competencies Model Based on Empirical Studies of the Competencies Clients and Legal Employers Want

At the center of the Foundational Competencies Model—visually and conceptually—is each student's internalization of a deep responsibility

21st Century Success: The Delta Lawyer Competency Model, THOMSON REUTERS (2019), https://legal.thomsonreuters.com/content/dam/ewp-m/documents/legal/en/pdf/white -papers/delta-lawyer-competency.pdf. See Hamilton & Bilionis, *supra* note 4, pages 9–10, for a more detailed explanation of how the Foundational Competencies Model builds off the Delta Model.

[9] "Competencies" is used here to include capacities and skills that legal employers and clients need.

and service orientation to others, especially the client, that creates trust. That internalized commitment informs all the other competencies. The center of the model also includes well-being practices because a lawyer must care for self in order to care for others.

The bottom side of the model makes clear that each student and lawyer must demonstrate the basic technical legal competencies that clients and employers need. Note that the 1L year is focused on these basic technical legal capacities and skills.

The left side of the model makes clear the foundational importance to clients and employers of each student and new lawyer demonstrating client-centered relational skills, problem-solving, and good professional judgment in serving the client—including superior client focus and responsiveness, exceptional understanding of the client's context and business, and communication skills including listening and knowing your audience.[10]

The right side of the model makes clear the foundational importance for clients and employers of ownership of continuous professional development (taking initiative) toward excellence at the competencies needed, harnessed to an entrepreneurial mindset to serve well in rapidly changing markets for both employers and clients. Employers and clients need strong skills of teamwork and collaboration, work ethic, conscientiousness and attention to detail, grit and resilience, and organization and management of legal work. An entrepreneurial mindset includes constant attention to client goals that the work be done more effectively and efficiently in changing markets, including making effective use of technology.

Note that in 2021 Bloomberg Law surveyed practicing attorneys and asked about the skills they wished new lawyers had learned before starting practice. The most needed were client communication and interaction skills. The practicing lawyers thought that good problem-solving and judgment were the most important characteristics of a successful attorney.

---

[10] Note that in the early years of practice for a new lawyer in a firm or law department, the "client" is essentially the experienced lawyer giving the new lawyer work.

3. Self-Assess Your Strengths

The third step is to self-assess the strengths you have with respect to the capacities and skills listed in Tables 1 and 2.

a. Self-Assess Your Strengths and Possible Areas for Improvement Regarding the Table 1 Technical Capacities and Skills

In this third step, you will first self-assess whether you have comparative strengths with respect to the traditional technical capacities and skills in Table 1. Your career services and academic support staff can help you with this assessment.

In the author's experience, law school culture generally sends messages that only the students ranking near the top of the class have a persuasive story that they have strengths regarding the first four of the Table 1 capacities and skills—knowledge of doctrinal law, legal analysis, legal research, and written and oral communication in the legal context. It is true that the larger law firms involved in on-campus interviewing usually emphasize a cutoff percentage with respect to overall rank when hiring students for their summer associate programs.[11] The medium and smaller firms and other types of legal employers do not generally have a class rank cutoff. They want an academic record that indicates strong probabilities of ultimate bar passage, plus the capacities and skills in Table 2. Remember that 90 percent of the practicing lawyers in your region were not in the top 10 percent of their law school class, and they understand that a law student who is going to pass the bar and has the capacities and skills in Table 2 is going to be an excellent lawyer serving clients well. If you are not in the top-ranked group in your class, you need to talk to practicing lawyers and judges who were also not in the top-ranked group in their classes. Ask how important their grades in law school have been to their success in the practice of law. Ask them if their class rank has been a factor after bar passage. Trust me, if you are in good standing at your law school, you have the Table 1 capacities and skills to provide excellent help as a law clerk.

---

[11] Note that post-graduation success on client development or a unique specialization that is in demand may open the door to later lateral opportunities in the big law firms.

In the author's experience, the key question to ask in the 1L year in terms of the Table 1 capacities and skills is whether the career services and academic support staff believe your grades in the required courses indicate a strong probability of bar passage. If so, you have a persuasive story that you are developing the necessary Table 1 capacities and skills to be an excellent law clerk. If your grades in these required doctrinal or lawyering skills courses indicate some risk with respect to bar passage, again relying on counsel from your career services and academic support staff, you need to work with them to create and implement a written professional development plan to improve your skills needed for bar passage. The fact that you have created and are implementing such a plan is a persuasive story of taking ownership over your professional development.

Remember that employers use grades as a predictor that you have the Table 1 skills necessary to be a good law clerk; once you have experiences where practicing lawyers or judges have seen your work and say that you can do the work well, then you have moved from a prediction that you can do the work to a demonstration that you can do the work well. When you ultimately pass the bar, your class rank is of diminishing importance, if any, except for entry-level positions with the bigger law firms and appellate clerkships. You do not know where your dentist, doctor, or nurse ranked in their class. You know they are licensed and you know whether they demonstrate the capacities and skills in Table 2 that justify your trust in them.

For those students seeking employment in larger firms with a class rank cutoff for their summer associate and associate programs, note that the pool of students who make the class rank cutoff is still large and the Table 2 capacities and skills will be the deciding factors to differentiate you.

b. Self-Assess Your Strengths Regarding the Table 2 Capacities and Skills

Now turn to self-assessing your strengths with respect to the capacities and skills in Table 2. You need to reflect on your past work and service experiences helping others, for example as a server, salesperson, team member, or team leader. Note that the capacities and skills of this sort that you developed earlier are all transferable to legal work. The template will ask you to select the four capacities and skills from Table 3 where you have the greatest strengths and rank them from 1 to 4.

Table 3 Assessment of Your Strengths Regarding the Capacities and Skills That Clients and Legal Employers Want in the Context of Your Previous Work/Service with Customers/Persons Served, Including Work on Teams

Capacities and Skills	Rank Your Top Four in Order (1–4)
1. Superior focus and responsiveness to the customers/persons served	
2. Exceptional understanding of the context and business of the customers/persons served	
3. Effective communication skills, including listening and knowing your audience	
4. Creative problem-solving and good professional judgment	
5. Ownership over continuous professional development (taking initiative) of all of the capacities and skills needed to serve well	
6. Teamwork and collaboration	
7. Strong work ethic	
8. Conscientiousness and attention to detail	
9. Grit and resilience	
10. Organization and management of the work (project management)	
11. An entrepreneurial mindset to serve customers/persons served more effectively and efficiently in changing markets	

Since we know that proactively seeking feedback on a self-assessment of strengths and reflecting on the feedback are critically important habits for continuous professional development, Step 3 of the template asks you to request one person (Person A), and ideally two people (Person A and Person B), who knows your earlier work/service to others well to fill out an assessment like Table 4. Holloran Center has Table 4 available at the link in the footnote.[12]

---

[12] *Table 4 from Chapter 1*, St. Thomas Sch. of L., https://law.stthomas.edu/about/centers -institutes/holloran-center/research-training/employment-roadmap/index.html (scroll down to "Third Edition Supplemental Materials"; link in bar at left) (last visited June 12, 2023).

Table 4 Ask Person A and ideally a second person, Person B, who know your earlier work/service well to rank your top four strengths in terms of the capacities and skills that clients and legal employers want in the context of your previous work/service with customers/persons served, including work on teams.

Assessment of _____ **(student name)**

Capacities and Skills	Rank the Student's Top Four in Order (1–4)
1. Superior focus and responsiveness to the customers/persons served	
2. Exceptional understanding of the context and business of the customers/persons served	
3. Effective communication skills, including listening and knowing your audience	
4. Creative problem-solving and good professional judgment	
5. Ownership over continuous professional development (taking initiative) of all of the capacities and skills needed to serve well	
6. Teamwork and collaboration	
7. Strong work ethic	
8. Conscientiousness and attention to detail	
9. Grit and resilience	
10. Organization and management of the work (project management)	
11. An entrepreneurial mindset to serve customers/persons served more effectively and efficiently in changing markets	

The online template then asks you, after reflecting on the feedback from Persons A and B, whether you want to modify your ranking of your four strongest capacities and skills in Table 3.

4. Evidence Supporting Your Four Strengths

The online template's fourth step asks you to consider evidence that future employers will value indicating your progression to a later stage of development on the four strongest capacities and skills you selected in Table 3. A first question is how would you know you are at a later stage of development on these strengths?

The Holloran Center at the University of St. Thomas (Minnesota) has created stage-development models, called Milestone Models, on some of the Table 2 capacities and skills. These Milestone Models can help you self-assess your stage of development on a capacity or skill and then help you identify the evidence you have supporting your self-assessment. For example, assume you have had significant earlier experience as a server or a salesperson, and you chose as a strength "superior focus and responsiveness to the customers/persons served" and/or "exceptional understanding of the context and business of the customers/persons served." The Professional Communication Milestone in Table 5 will be helpful in your self-assessment of your stage of development.

The Holloran Center website has additional Milestone Models on Client-Centered Problem-Solving and Good Judgment, Active Listening, Ownership of Continuous Professional Development, Teamwork and Collaboration, and Grit and Resilience. They can be found at this link: https://law.stthomas.edu/about/centers-institutes/holloran-center/learning-outcomes-database/index.html

What is good evidence that employers value? A 2016 study (with responses from 24,000 lawyers) asked respondents what criteria were most helpful in the decision to hire an attorney. Table 6 has the 13 most helpful criteria.[13]

---

[13] ALLI GERKMAN & LOGAN CORNETT, FOUNDATIONS FOR PRACTICE: HIRING THE WHOLE LAWYER: EXPERIENCE MATTERS 7–8 (2016).

Table 5 Holloran Center Milestone Model on Professional Communication[14]

Sub-competency	Novice	Intermediate	Competent	Exceptional
Purposeful The communicator is **purposeful** in identifying specific goals for the communication and in choosing and competently using a medium/platform(s) and effecting a tone and behaviors best suited to achieving the goal(s). Additionally, the communicator is attentive and responsive to recipients, adopting medium, tone, behaviors, and content to most effectively and appropriately engage in exchange with recipients.	The communicator is rarely purposeful.	The communicator is sometimes purposeful.	The communicator is usually purposeful.	The communicator is consistently purposeful.
Clear The communicator is **clear**, choosing words, construction, and concepts precisely, and organizing them concisely, to most effectively convey the information intended without wordiness or redundancy and using words and concepts that are likely to be understandable to reasonably foreseen recipient(s).	The communicator is rarely clear.	The communicator is sometimes clear.	The communicator is usually clear.	The communicator is consistently clear.

---

[14] Professional Communication Working Group members are Erin Binns (Marquette), Elyse Diamond (Pace), Quiche Suzuki (New Mexico).

Sub-competency	Novice	Intermediate	Competent	Exceptional
Accurate The communicator is **accurate**, exchanging information with attentiveness to detail and with an ethical honesty that is error free and implements best practices in format and structure for communicating on the chosen medium/platform.	The communicator is rarely accurate.	The communicator is sometimes accurate.	The communicator is usually accurate.	The communicator is consistently accurate.
Aware The communicator is **aware**, exercising good judgment and making deliberate choices in content, form, and delivery that aim to be without bias, prejudice, or assumptions and demonstrate awareness of and respect for the relationship between the communicator and recipient; the personal, cultural, and professional identity of the recipient; and the conventions and expectations of the applicable organization/industry /employer/school/recipient.	The communicator is rarely aware.	The communicator is sometimes aware.	The communicator is usually aware.	The communicator is consistently aware.

Table 6 The 13 Most Helpful Hiring Criteria for Employers Hiring Students for Post-Graduation Employment

Hiring Criteria	% of Respondents Answering "Somewhat Helpful" or "Very Helpful"
Legal employment	88.3%
Recommendations from practitioners or judges	81.9%
Legal externship	81.6%
Other experiential education	79.4%
Life experience between college and law school	78.3%
Participation in law school clinic	77.3%
Law school courses in a particular specialty	70.3%
Recommendations from professors	63.3%
Class rank	62.5%
Law school attended	61.1%
Extracurricular activities	58.7%
Ties to a particular geographic location	54.3%
Law review experience	51.2%

While this survey found that all the criteria were helpful in making a hiring decision, the six most helpful criteria are all related to practical experience. It is very important that you have evidence of your practical experiences that have been evaluated by experienced lawyers, judges, and professors who have seen your work in experiential situations.

Do your resume, your cover letter, and your reference letters all support your persuasive story about your strongest capacities and skills and how they benefit your target audience of employers? You should have in mind your best brief stories of when you successfully used or developed these strongest capacities and skills to the next level. For example, the author's experience is that employers will infer the capacities of initiative and strong work ethic from the following pieces of evidence on a resume or cover letter or from stories in an interview:

- Growing up on a family farm, especially with animals
- Working through school
- Achieving Eagle Scout status

- Serving in the military
- Demonstrating a record of initiative and seeking more responsibility in previous employment
- Working as a server or in a customer-facing job like sales
- Starting a business
- Excelling at sports or activities like debate
- Excelling at art or music
- Training for and completing a marathon
- Overcoming significant hardships/adversity

Consider creating a file where you collect the evidence you have of later-stage development of your strengths. A file is a simple way of organizing evidence of your hard work over the three years of law school and the years preceding law school. For example, the file should have your best stories that you can tell when someone asks a question about a capacity or skill, like "Tell me about a time when you showed [any of the capacities and skills in Table 2]" or "Tell me what you learned from [reference to an experience on your resume]." Remember that these questions are essentially asking you to tell the interviewer something about yourself that will benefit the interviewer's organization.

5. Make a Tentative Judgment about Where You Would Like to Get Employment/Service Experience in the Next Phase of Your Development

Step 5 of the online template asks you to reflect on Steps 1–4 and formulate a tentative judgment on where you find the best fit with respect to

a. the geographic region where you would like employment/service experience in this next phase of your development;
b. the most interesting areas of practice and type of client for you to explore; and
c. the type of employing organization you would like to join.

If you have little experience with the practice of law, this fifth step may seem very challenging. This step is by definition a tentative judgment that you will test by getting experience. However, you need the help of experienced attorneys, faculty, and staff to get the experiences you need for your discernment process. If you tell them some version of "I have no idea what I want to do," they don't know how to help you. In contrast, if you say some version of "I don't have a lot of experience, but I would like to try _____ [with respect to the previous items a. through c.]," a practicing attorney or a faculty or staff member can work to help you gain needed experience.

You might discover that a volunteer experience, part-time work experience, or practice area or employer you thought might be a good fit is not in fact a good fit. That's okay. You are moving forward on answering the discernment questions in Figure 1.

Remember that even if all of your initial tentative judgments about fit in terms of geography, practice area, type of client, and type of employing organization prove, after experience, not to be a good fit for you, you still have moved forward with respect to your professional capacities and skills in Tables 1 and 2. At your entry level of development, all these capacities and skills are transferable to other geographies, practice areas, client types, and organizational types. You are also demonstrating a later stage of ownership over your own professional development.

6. Take Ownership over Your Professional Development

Step 6 in the online template focuses specifically on your self-assessment of your stage of development on ownership of your own professional development. Fostering your growth to the next stage of development on this particular capacity is a central focus of the Roadmap process. Strong empirical data show that student growth toward later stages of ownership of continuous professional development enhances student academic performance[15] and that stronger student academic performance in turn

---

[15] "Research has amassed overwhelming evidence that ownership over your own professional development (self-regulated or self-directed learning in the scholarly literature) enhances student performance and achievement in courses and course units." Linda Nilson, Creating Self-Regulated Learners 10–11 (2013). "It has been shown that self-regulated learning is one of the best predictors of academic performance" and "self-regulated learners are more effective learners." Susanna Lucieer et al., *Self-Regulated Learning and Academic Performance in Medical Education*, 38 Med. Tchr. 585, 586 (2016). Self-regulated activity "has consistently been found to be related to student achievement."

correlates with higher probabilities of bar passage.[16] Empirical data show that employers strongly value this capacity, and a student at a later stage of development will have higher probabilities of meaningful employment. Korn Ferry, the largest executive recruiting firm in the world, concludes from its research that "continuous life-long learning is the number one determinant of a person's earnings for life."[17]

The Roadmap online template will ask you to choose the stage of development where you are now on this Milestone Model in Table 7.

Remember that you should self-assess at a particular stage of development on Table 7 only if you can answer an interviewer's question, "What evidence do you have to support your self-assessment regarding ownership over professional development?" You can see that having a file of your best stories on this or any other capacity/skill you are emphasizing will greatly help your persuasive argument.

7. Create a Tentative Written Professional Development Plan

Step 7 in the online Roadmap template will ask you to map out a tentative written plan to use your remaining time in law school to gain the experiences you need to test your tentative judgments from Step 5 about the best fit for you. Remember that the best "rotational"-type experiences, whether inside or outside of the building, will mimic the actual work of lawyers, especially in the practice area of most interest to you.

Renee Jansen et al., *Self-Regulated Learning Partially Mediates the Effect of Self-Regulated Learning Interventions on Achievement in Higher Education: A Meta-Analysis*, 28 Educ. Rsch. Rev. 1, 2 (2019). "Students who were willing to reflect and make changes in their learning strategies and who selected active strategies that inherently involved regulating their learning were more likely to have academic success." Jennifer Gundlach & Jessica Santangelo, *Teaching and Assessing Metacognition in Law School*, 69 J. Legal Educ. 156, 180 (2019).

[16] *See* Linda F. Wightman, Law Sch. Admission Counsel, LSAC National Longitudinal Bar Passage Study 37 (1998); Douglas Rush & Hisako Matsuo, *Does Law School Curriculum Affect Bar Examination Passage? An Empirical Analysis of Factors Related to Bar Examination Passage during the Years 2001 through 2006 at a Midwestern Law School*, 57 J. Legal Educ. 224, 232–33 (2007); Katherine A. Austin, Catherine Martin Christopher & Darby Dickerson, *Will I Pass the Bar Exam?: Predicting Student Success Using LSAT Scores and Law School Performance*, 45 Hofstra L. Rev. 253, 266–68 (2017).

[17] Gary Burnison, Lose the Resume, Land the Job 56–57 (2018).

Table 7 Holloran Center Milestone Model on Assessment of Student's Ownership of Continuous Professional Development (Self-Directedness)

Sub-competencies of Ownership/Self-Directedness	Novice Learner (Level 1)	Intermediate Learner (Level 2)	Competent Learner (Level 3)	Exceptional Learner (Level 4)
1. Self-Assesses and Identifies Strengths and Areas for Growth *Understands full range of lawyering competencies and diagnoses learning needs*[18]	RARELY demonstrates understanding of full range of lawyering competencies and diagnoses learning needs	SOMETIMES demonstrates understanding of full range of lawyering competencies and diagnoses learning needs	OFTEN demonstrates understanding of full range of lawyering competencies and diagnoses learning needs	CONSISTENTLY demonstrates understanding of full range of lawyering competencies and diagnoses learning needs
2. Articulates Goals and Follows a Plan *Implements a written professional development plan reflecting goals that are specific, measurable, achievable, relevant, and time-bound*[18]	RARELY creates and implements a written professional development plan reflecting goals that are specific, measurable, achievable, relevant, and time-bound	SOMETIMES creates and implements a written professional development plan reflecting goals that are specific, measurable, achievable, relevant, and time-bound	OFTEN creates and implements a written professional development plan reflecting goals that are specific, measurable, achievable, relevant, and time-bound	CONSISTENTLY creates and implements a written professional development plan reflecting goals that are specific, measurable, achievable, relevant, and time-bound

[18] Goals that exhibit these factors are referred to as SMART Goals: Specific—clear goals including what, why, and how; Measurable—including a clear method for evaluation of progress; Achievable—including obstacles and realistic solutions; Relevant—including connection to core values; and

Sub-competencies of Ownership/Self-Directedness	Novice Learner (Level 1)	Intermediate Learner (Level 2)	Competent Learner (Level 3)	Exceptional Learner (Level 4)
3. Acquires and Learns from Experience *Seeks experiences to develop competencies and meet articulated goals, and seeks and incorporates feedback received during the experiences*	RARELY seeks experiences and seeks and incorporates feedback received during the experiences	SOMETIMES seeks experiences and seeks and incorporates feedback received during the experiences	OFTEN seeks experiences and seeks and incorporates feedback received during the experiences	CONSISTENTLY seeks experiences and seeks and incorporates feedback received during the experiences
4. Reflects and Applies Lessons Learned *Uses reflective practice[19] to reflect on performance, contemplate lessons learned, identify how to apply lessons learned to improve in the future, and applies those lessons*	RARELY uses reflective practice to reflect on performance, contemplate lessons learned, identify how to apply lessons learned to improve in the future, and applies those lessons	SOMETIMES uses reflective practice to reflect on performance, contemplate lessons learned, identify how to apply lessons learned to improve in the future, and applies those lessons	OFTEN uses reflective practice to reflect on performance, contemplate lessons learned, identify how to apply lessons learned to improve in the future, and applies those lessons	CONSISTENTLY uses reflective practice to reflect on performance, contemplate lessons learned, identify how to apply lessons learned to improve in the future, and applies those lessons

Time-bound—including a clear timeline of steps.

[19] Reflective practice requires learners to focus on their own performance (what?); consider multiple perspectives, including their own, and contemplate lessons learned (so what?); and identify how to apply lessons learned to improve in the future (now what?).

Your tentative written professional development plan also maps out how to develop your strongest capacities and skills from Step 3 to the next level and how to create even stronger evidence of your development (Step 4). Step 7 also contributes to your story of later-stage ownership over your own professional development (Step 6).

The main goals in planning for the summer after your 1L year, your 2L year, the summer after your 2L year, and your 3L year are to

1. Gain experience that will test whether your top areas of interest for employment are a good fit for you;
2. Grow toward later stages of development with respect to your strongest competencies;
3. Obtain persuasive evidence that your target employers will accept regarding your growth in the previous item and your value proposition to them; and
4. Ensure that you meet your school's graduation requirements and maximize the probability that you pass the bar examination.

How far out in terms of summers and semesters a student can effectively do a written professional development plan will vary depending on how much experience a student has prior to law school and the opportunities a student may have because of existing professional relationships. For example, some students early in the second semester of their 1L year may already have summer employment lined up for the summer between their 1L and 2L years. Some students with family relationships may already have offers of post-graduation employment. A student at the beginning of the second semester of the 1L year who does not have a good summer experience lined up for the coming summer should focus early in the spring semester on securing summer experience and then on a plan for registration for the first semester of the 2L year plus other non-curricular experiences in that first semester of the 2L year. A 1L student who already has summer employment lined up for the first summer or even post-graduation employment should (1) use the Roadmap process to develop a written professional development plan for the student's remaining time in law school that the student shows to future employers; (2) get feedback from them; and (3) reflect on the feedback. Note that an employer may want such a student to get experience in a variety of practice areas with several different kinds of clients.

a. Focus First on the Summer between Your 1L and 2L Years

Your goal is to get paid or unpaid experience to test one or more of the three tentative judgments you made regarding your best fit in Step 5. You also want experience and feedback on experience to grow toward later stages of development on any of your top four competencies and skills from Step 3 and to have evidence to support your persuasive story about your strengths (Step 4).

Do you have paid or unpaid summer experience between the 1L and 2L years lined up at this point? If not, this is an important priority for you in the spring semester of the 1L year. See career services to get feedback on your resume and your strategy. See Step 9 on using your natural networks and building professional relationships that help you reach your goals.

After your summer experience, reflect on the feedback and the experiences from the summer with respect to your fit and your growth toward later stages of your strengths. Based on those reflections, revise your Roadmap plan.

b. Focus Next on the Fall and Spring of Your 2L Year

Seek experiences both inside and outside the law school with the same goal as in the previous section. Inside the law school, consider carefully the experiential courses including externships, internships, and simulation courses like Negotiation, ADR, Practicum courses, or Client Interviewing and Counseling, all of which can be very useful in supporting your discernment process. Consider especially the clinics. Consider activities like Moot Court. Are there doctrinal courses that also involve doing the work of a practicing lawyer like drafting documents?

Be strategic with experiences outside of the formal curriculum in your remaining time in law school. How will those experiences help you grow to the next stage of development in the competencies you are emphasizing? What evidence will those experiences provide to show that you are at a later stage of development for a particular competency? Experiences outside the formal curriculum include but are not limited to clerkships (paid or unpaid); pro bono and service work; student organizations; and work with the organized bar. Rather than create a laundry list of such activities, think strategically about activities that will be the most effective evidence of growth at one of your strongest competencies. For example, if one of your strongest competencies is project management in teams, seek a leadership position in a student organization and define a specific new project that the team can accomplish in a specific time period. Is it possible for an experienced lawyer/judge/professor/staff member (perhaps an advisor to the student organization) to vouch for your achievement? Creating and implementing a written plan to build professional relationships (Step 9 of the Roadmap process) also is very important to help you develop long-term relationships with experienced professors, staff, lawyers, and judges who observe and can speak to your strongest competencies.

Finally, think strategically about which two professors you will ask for references, and be certain to take enough classes or gain enough other experiences with each of them so they both have substantial evidence of your strongest competencies. Also, think strategically about relationships and references from two experienced lawyers/judges outside of the law school who will have substantial evidence of your strongest competencies. Ideally, you will have two excellent inside references and two excellent outside references who have good evidence of your strongest competencies by the end of your fourth semester of law school. Chapter 4, Step 4 has a further discussion of the importance of developing relationships with professors in the 1L and 2L years.

Reflect on the feedback and the experiences from each semester of the 2L year with respect to your fit and your growth toward later stages of your strengths. Revise your Roadmap plan.

c. Consider Next the Summer between the 2L and 3L Years

The experiences from your summer between the 1L and 2L years and the experiences of the 2L year may substantially affect your goals, so if you are completing your plan in the spring semester of the 1L year, this part of your Roadmap plan may be highly tentative and brief. Reflect on the feedback and the experiences from the summer with respect to your fit and your growth toward later stages of your strengths. Revise.

d. Consider Next the Fall and Spring of the 3L Year

The experiences from your two summers and the experiences of the 2L year may substantially affect your goals, so this part of your Roadmap plan may be highly tentative and brief. Reflect on the feedback and the experiences from the summer with respect to your fit and your growth toward later stages of your strengths. Revise.

With respect to the goal of ensuring you meet graduation requirements and maximizing the probability that you pass the bar examination, first go through all the graduation requirements and map out in writing the next four semesters and two summers of law school. In what specific semesters and summers will you complete the graduation requirements? Consider also the prerequisites for the upper-level elective courses you want to take and how often these electives are offered so that you have the proper sequence of courses during your 2L and 3L years.

Note that many law schools have an upper-level writing requirement. Seriously consider doing the upper-level paper (or a long paper in a seminar) in the third or fourth semester of law school so that you have a strong example (and evidence from your supervising professor) of your research, writing, and analytical competencies to show potential employers. If you meet all deadlines with good-quality work product, this is also an example of good project management. If you are applying for appellate clerkships, then by March of your 2L year, you should have one or two longer written projects as evidence of your research and writing and analytical competencies.

Next write down all the subjects that are tested in the state where you intend to take the bar examination. Decide whether you will take a course on all of the bar examination subjects or nearly all of them (and leave a few bar examination subjects to be covered by the bar review course and your independent study). Seek counsel on these choices from your law school's academic support staff person or a knowledgeable student services professional. The staff person will have the best judgment on whether you should take a course in all of the bar examination subjects and, if you decide not to do so, which bar examination subjects are less difficult to study on your own.

Note that if you are ranked in the lowest quartile of your class at many law schools, you likely have a higher probability of failing the bar examination. You need the counsel of an academic support person to draft a written plan of how to use your remaining time in law school most effectively to improve your knowledge, analytical skills, and communication skills to maximize your probability of passing the bar. Seriously consider taking a course on each of the bar examination subjects.

You should add to your written map of the next four semesters and two summers when you will take courses on the bar examination subjects.

8. Practice Your Persuasive Story to Potential Employers

Essentially, you are lawyering for yourself to make a short persuasive argument that will convince a target audience of your most promising employers that you add value to the employer. Remember that versions of common questions like "Tell me about yourself" or "Why did you go to law school?" are really "Tell me something about yourself in about one to two minutes that will benefit my organization" or "Do any of your briefly stated reasons for going to law school indicate that you will add value to my organization?" From an employer's standpoint, if you cannot make a brief persuasive argument for yourself in this context, how effective will you be making persuasive arguments on behalf of clients?

Step 8 of the online template asks you to formulate a persuasive story that several of your strengths from Step 3 will benefit your target-audience listener. In a one- to two-minute answer to a specific question, you really have time only to make two or three main points that your listener will remember. The listener will usually follow up with a question to ask you for more information on one or more of your key points. Be ready with your "A" story, your "B" story, and so on that provide strong evidence to support your main points. Create a file of your best stories.

One key persuasive story to consider is whether you can communicate a strong passion or strong positive energy to serve the types of clients and do the kind of work that the target employer has. For example, if you are seeking a social justice position, you must communicate passion and positive energy to serve the disadvantaged, and you will need examples of how you have done this service in the past.

It is extremely helpful, even if it feels awkward, to practice these short persuasive stories with others who can give you feedback. Do you keep good eye contact? Do you use voice and facial expression variation for emphasis? Do you use your hands for emphasis? In a Zoom context, do you have good lighting and a camera angle showing the upper part of your body, and do you bring your hands for emphasis up high enough for the viewer to see them?

9. Develop Your Plan to Build a Tent of Professional Relationships

Every successful lawyer in any practice context has built a tent of relationships with professionals based on trust that help the lawyer both to achieve his or her goals and to influence others on behalf of the lawyer's clients. Similarly, you need to build a tent of relationships with professionals based on trust that will help you achieve your immediate goal of finding experiences that enable you to discern your passion, motivating interests, and strengths that best fit with a practice area/type of client and employer.

Given all of your other responsibilities in law school, you are short on time, and you need to be strategic in using your available time to achieve your professional relationship goals. You need a written plan to build a tent of professional relationships that flows from the written professional development plan. This is a transferable skill that will be helpful in a wide array of contexts. Chapter 4 explains the steps you should take to build a tent of relationships with professionals who both support you and trust you to do the work of a lawyer.

10. Practice Your Habit of Proactively Seeking Feedback, Reflecting, and Revising Your Plans

Some law schools provide you with a coach who will give you feedback on your Roadmap template plan. This is an exceptionally helpful resource. If your school does not provide a coach, it is critically important for you to be proactive in seeking a lawyer or judge who will spend 45 minutes giving you feedback. Then reflect on the feedback and revise your plan. Your career services team should be able to help you achieve this step.

The Roadmap process is iterative. During and after each significant experience, proactively seek feedback, reflect, and revise your Roadmap plan. What did you learn from each experience? If you change your Roadmap plan, then also revisit and revise your written plan to build a tent of professional relationships. This reflection and revision habit after each significant work experience will be extremely valuable going forward in your career.

Assume that after one or more experiences, you decide to change your Roadmap plan in terms of geographic area, area of practice or type of client, or type of employer. It is important for you to see that in this process of implementing your Roadmap template plan, including changing your priorities after reflection on experience, you are demonstrating a later stage of development on the foundational capacity in Table 7 of ownership over your continuous professional development. As a law student and early career lawyer, all the Table 1 and Table 2 basic capacities and skills you are learning in these experiences are transferable to other practice areas, types of client, and types of employer.

Indiana Law professor William Henderson emphasizes that the "A" players in a law firm's talent management systems "typically earn that designation because of their self-directed ability to continuously learn and adapt."[20] In conversations about associates in large firms, senior lawyers focus on the degree to which an associate goes "above and beyond" in taking ownership over the associate's projects and his or her role on the team and in the firm itself.

An empirical study of lawyers who made partner in a firm in contrast to those who did not found that the lawyers who made partner "were masters of their fate; they tend to strategically plan both their day-to-day work and their careers. As a group, they tend to make and stick to plans more than lawyers who did not make partner."[21] Fast-tracking partners "are more likely to 'tune' their plans as they encounter new information. They seek out constructive feedback and use it to improve their work."[22]

---

[20] William Henderson, *Talent Systems for Law Firms*, PRO. DEV. Q. 1, 7 (Feb. 2017).

[21] LORI BERMAN ET AL., ACCELERATING LAWYER SUCCESS: HOW TO MAKE PARTNER, STAY HEALTHY, AND FLOURISH IN A LAW FIRM 7–8 (2016).

[22] *Id.* at 26.

The same study concludes, "Flourishing is also enabled by something we call 'focused ownership'—taking initiative and ownership to solve problems and accomplish goals."[23]

---

[23] *Id.* at 29.

CHAPTER 2

COMPLETING THE ONLINE ROADMAP TEMPLATE

https://law.stthomas.edu/about/centers-institutes/holloran-center
/research-training/employment-roadmap/index.html

Please read Chapter 1 first. You may need to refer to Chapter 1 for longer descriptions of some of the steps in this template. After you have finished, be sure to go on to read Chapters 3 and 4.

This template focuses on your plan to gain a breadth of experiences during your remaining time in law school so that you can

1. thoughtfully discern your passion, motivating interests, and strengths that best fit with a geographic community of practice, a practice area and type of client, and type of employer;
2. develop your strengths to the next level; and
3. have evidence of your strengths that employers value.

If you already have post-graduation employment, fill out the Roadmap template with an eye toward your capacities and skills that will most benefit your employer and its clients. What experiences will help you develop those capacities and skills to the next level? Show your plan to experienced lawyers at your future employer and ask for feedback. Reflect on the feedback.

Fill in the template with reasonably brief answers. You can use bullet points. Remember that the coaches who will help you with feedback will have time to read only reasonably brief answers. Include your resume when you send this template to a coach for feedback.

Roadmap Template

Name of Student: _____

Step 1—Assess your passion and motivating interests in employment.
Think about the three most memorable days/weeks giving you the most positive meaning and energy in your work or service experiences.

1. **Whom were you helping?**
   a. _____
   b. _____
   c. _____

2. **To do what?**
   a. _____
   b. _____
   c. _____

3. **What specific capacities and skills were you using in the work/service that yielded positive meaning and energy for you?**
   a. _____
   b. _____
   c. _____

Step 2—Understand the full range of capacities and skills legal employers and clients need.
Look carefully at Tables 1 and 2 in Chapter 1.

Step 3—Self-assess your strengths.

a.   The traditional technical competencies that law schools emphasize.
Focus on the first four competencies in Table 1 in Chapter 1. The career services and academic support staff at your school will be able to help you assess whether your performance in the 1L required courses gives you a persuasive story that you are comparatively strong at these capacities and skills or in the alternative whether you have a story of solid performance that indicates strong probabilities that you will pass the bar exam. If your grade in any 1L required course was low (talk to your career services and academic support staff to assess what is a grade indicating bar passage

risk, but in general the bottom 20 percent in a course), consider creating and implementing a written professional development plan with guided reflection from academic support to improve the skills you need to pass the bar.

With respect to the first four competencies in Table 1, I have
   1. a story of comparative strength at _____

_____;
   2. a story of solid performance at _____

_____;
   3. a plan to improve the skills I need to pass the bar with respect to

_____.

b.   The non-technical capacities and skills in Table 3 in Chapter 1.
My top four capacities and skills from Table 3 are
   1. _____
   2. _____
   3. _____
   4. _____

I have asked two different people who know my earlier work/service to fill out Table 4 and have reflected on their assessment. Based on their feedback and my reflection, I will make the following changes (if any) to my top four capacities and skills:

Step 4—What evidence supports your four strengths?
For each of your four strengths, indicate your best two stories from your earlier work/service including college that show you are at a later stage of development on that strength.
   Strength 1:_____ and _____.
   Strength 2:_____ and _____.
   Strength 3:_____ and _____.
   Strength 4:_____ and _____.

Step 5—Make a tentative judgment about where you would like to get employment/service experience in the next phase of your development. Reflecting on your answers to the previous Steps 1–4, make a tentative judgment about where you would like to get employment/service experience in this next phase of your development. Note that the focus here is on your top two choices so that your current efforts are focused and you are able to give guidance to experienced lawyers who are trying to help you. There may be other areas of interest down the road that you can include as you gain experience and revise your Roadmap plan.

a. **Top geographic regions:** (1) _____ and (2) _____.

b. **Top areas of practice/type of client:** (1) _____ and (2) _____.

c. **Top type of employing organization:** (1) _____ and (2) _____.

Step 6—What is your developmental stage regarding ownership over your professional development?

Look at Table 7 in Chapter 1 on ownership of continuous professional development.

Select a stage of development and write it on the following lines only if you have good evidence (stories) to offer when an interviewer asks you, "What evidence do you have that you are at the stage of development that you selected?"

1. Stage of development on "self-assesses and identifies strengths and areas for growth": _____.

2. Stage of development on "articulates goals and follows a written plan": _____.

3. Stage of development on "acquires and learns from experience": _____.

4. Stage of development on "reflects and applies lessons learned": _____.

Step 7—Create a tentative plan to gain experiences, both inside and outside the building, during your remaining time in law school that mimic as much as possible the work the lawyers do in the areas of your best "fit" regarding employment identified in Step 5 and that help you develop your strengths identified in Step 3 to the next level and have evidence of your growth.

Summer experience between the 1L and 2L years.
Do you have summer experience already lined up? If so, where?

_____

If not, what specific steps on what specific timetable are you taking to line up good summer experience? _____

_____

_____

You will be registering for the fall semester of your 2L year in the spring of your 1L year. What experience do you want in the fall of your 2L year inside the building? _____

_____

Experience outside the building? _____

_____

Step 8—Practice your persuasive story to your top-priority potential employers.
Assume you are in a 20-minute screening interview with one of your top-priority potential employers who starts the interview by saying "Tell me why we should hire you."

Briefly list the top two points you want to make in your persuasive story that you meet the employer's needs. Assume you will have no more than two minutes to make these two points with one short supporting story on each one.

1.   _____

2.   _____

Step 9—Outline two concrete steps with a timetable for the remainder of the 1L year and the summer between the 1L and 2L years to build a tent of professional relationships that will help you both to have good evidence of your strengths from Steps 3 and 4 and to achieve your goals in Step 7. Chapters 4 and 5 will help you develop a more complete written professional relationships plan.

1.   Do you have one or two professors who have seen your work and can speak to your Step 3 and Step 4 strengths? List them. _____ _____ If not, what is your plan to develop this type of relationship? _____
2.   Do you have one or two lawyers or judges outside of the building who have seen your work and can speak to your Step 3 and Step 4 strengths? List them. _____ If not, what is your plan to develop this type of relationship? _____

_____

Step 10—Developing your habit of proactively seeking experience and feedback, reflecting on it, and continuously revising and improving your Roadmap professional development plan.

In the spring of the 1L year, you should ask an experienced lawyer/judge to go over your Roadmap template and give you feedback. Based on your experiences in the summer between your 1L and 2L years, you will revisit this Roadmap plan again with an experienced lawyer/judge to reflect on your summer experience, discern the changes you want to make in the Roadmap template, and then plan for experience in the spring semester of your 2L year, the summer between the 2L and 3L years, and experience in the 3L year. In this process, you are going to develop to a later stage with respect to Table 7's Milestone Model on Assessment of Student's Ownership of Continuous Professional Development.

CHAPTER 3

YOUR TIMELINE FOR THE ROADMAP PROCESS[24]

This chapter provides a general timeline of steps related to your Roadmap process. Use it as a checklist to help you navigate your way through your three years of law school and to create evidence of your commitment to professional development. Keep in mind, however, that professional development is an ongoing project that will continue after you have finished law school.

In addition to following the timeline next, it is important to review and update your Roadmap after you have significant experiences that provide information regarding the answers to the four questions relating to your goals.

1. **1L Fall Semester**

- Receive and read through this timeline for Roadmap steps.
- Understand the competencies that legal employers and clients want. Determine which competencies are the focuses of required 1L curriculum and which competencies you should develop in the

---

[24] Authored by Neil W. Hamilton, Carl J.L. Numrich, Bryan M. Wachter, Christopher Damian, Sean Smallwood, and Robert Rohloff.

elective curriculum and other experiences of law school.

- Explore various organizations, volunteer opportunities, and campus events with an eye toward developing the important competencies.
- Update your resume and schedule a meeting with your school's office of career and professional development after October 15.
- Reflect on your strengths, weaknesses, and values. Begin discerning what direction you are headed and how you will get there.
- Seek out upperclassmen and practicing attorneys for advice, recommendations, and tips as you navigate your first year.
- Begin forging a relationship with a professor who knows your work well enough to write you a letter of recommendation after your first year.
- Create and implement a plan to build a tent of professional relationships.
- **Explore your interests and engage in the profession through joining bar association and affinity bar mentorship programs. Some application processes close before winter break.**
- **Become familiar with your law school's job bank site, such as Symplicity. You can begin applying for summer positions in December.**

Key Transition Point: Early Job Fair Deadlines

Specialty legal areas, such as intellectual property, and certain diversity job fair applications close in early December. Meet with your coach or career services personnel prior to completing applications.

Key Transition Point: Results from Fall Grades

Regardless of your feelings about your results, this is an important time to reflect on what went well and what can be adjusted in the future. Meet with your coach or career services personnel to discuss the semester and get tips moving forward.

2. **1L Spring Semester**
   - Complete the Roadmap template and discuss your plan for employment with a senior advisor.
   - Continue exploring various organizations, volunteer opportunities, and campus events. Commit yourself to an on-campus organization and seek out leadership, project management, and teamwork experiences.
   - Continue updating your resume.
   - Research and seek out employment/volunteer/research opportunities for the summer after your 1L year that will help you both explore your most promising employment options and develop the competencies on which you want to focus. Ask professors if they need summer help. Meet with your career services office to learn about upcoming application deadlines that may interest you.

   > **Key Transition Point: Roadmap**
   >
   > After finishing your Roadmap, be sure to check in, debrief, and discuss future goals with your coach or career services personnel.

   - **Consider your summer options early and often. Many 1L opportunities are unpaid. Begin looking for summer funding early, and consider any externship opportunities offered through your school.**
   - Register for classes for the following semester that will highlight the competencies you want to emphasize.
   - Continue forging a relationship with a professor who could write you a letter of recommendation after your first year and begin forging a similar relationship with another faculty member who knows your strongest competencies.
   - Continue updating and implementing your plan to build a tent of professional relationships and try other networking opportunities in areas of interest compatible with your areas of interest.
   - Run for an executive position for an on-campus organization in which you could demonstrate project management and teamwork competency skills.

- Look carefully at the bar examination subjects in the state where you intend to take the bar. *Note that an increasing number of states are moving to the Uniform Bar Examination. Decide whether you want to take a course on each bar subject.*

> **Key Transition Point: Selecting 2L Courses**
>
> Before registration reflect upon and update your Roadmap. Be sure to include classes supporting your value proposition.

- Before registration for the fall semester, plan out the sequence of courses in your last four semesters, including prerequisites.

3. **1L–2L Summer**

   a. June (Prior to Beginning of 2L Year)

- Research and familiarize yourself with legal employers in the geographic region in which you wish to work.
- Reach out to attorneys in areas of law that interest you to schedule informational interviews over the summer. Implement your plan to build a tent of professional relationships in general.
- Decide whether you will participate in on-campus interviewing (OCI). If you are considering OCI, then check with your career services office on the timetable and deadlines.
- Finalize your summer plans to gain legal experience. If you have already begun your summer work, make sure you are turning in good work and building trusting relationships with your colleagues and supervisors. You need, at minimum, one supervisor who really knows your work and strongest competencies.
- Research and familiarize yourself with summer job fairs in geographic or practice areas that interest you and make note of upcoming summer deadlines. Many off-campus job fairs have application deadlines in early summer and conduct interviews in July and August.

   b. July (Prior to Beginning of 2L Year)

   If you intend to participate in OCI:

- Research the legal employers participating in OCI.
- Discuss the OCI process with your school's office of career and professional development, taking note of important dates and procedures.

- Create or update your resume.
- Create and carefully proofread cover letters for target employers.
- Select writing samples, making sure to secure permission if using a sample from a work or volunteer project.
- Prepare references.
- Generate an unofficial transcript.
- Convert all files to PDF format.
- Meet someone at your school to review your application materials.
- Schedule a mock interview.
- Meet with attorneys to whom you reached out in June.
- Attend networking events hosted by firms participating in OCI.
- Attend off-campus job fairs applied for in June.
- Continue researching and familiarizing yourself with legal employers in the geographic region and general field of law in which you wish to work. Consider getting lists of alumni from your undergraduate institution and alumni from your law school who are lawyers in that region and field of law.

c. August (Prior to Beginning of 2L Year)

- Meet with attorneys you reached out to in June.
- If you are participating in OCIs, take note of important deadlines. Ensure that you have gathered and reviewed all necessary documents.
- Update your resume to reflect any legal work or coursework you completed during the summer.
- Continue researching and familiarizing yourself with legal employers in the geographic region and field of law in which you wish to work.

> **Key Transition Point: Reflect on Summer Experience**
>
> Which of your top employment options have you confirmed or eliminated? Did you grow to a later developmental stage on any competency? What evidence do you have regarding growth to a later stage of your strongest competency?

- Select an assignment from your 1L year that could be used as a writing sample. Take the time to review it and polish it if possible. Consider having a mentor or other senior lawyer review the document for you.
- Review your law school's job bank for fall experience opportunities.

4. **2L Fall Semester**

a. Ongoing over the 2L Year

- Select an upper-level paper topic that helps you demonstrate competencies for the area of employment you want. Do the upper-level paper early enough in law school so that it is both useful as a basis for discussion with potential employers and a good example of your writing ability and overall implementation of your Roadmap. Also, completing an upper-level paper earlier during your law-school career provides you with a potential source for a letter of recommendation from a professor who will know your writing skills and project management skills well. Consider a plan where you develop at least two strong references from two professors about your research, writing, and project management skills by doing an upper-level writing requirement for two credits with one professor and then another two-credit supervised research with another professor.

- If you are planning on applying for appellate-level judicial clerkships in the summer after your 2L year, expedite your plan to have two strong references from professors and your plan to have strong writing samples. Consider taking multiple classes with the same professor, taking classes with smaller class sizes, or working as a research assistant to a professor to help build relationships with professors.

- Seek out opportunities in the curriculum to develop portfolios of experiences in the competencies you wish to emphasize. Ask professors for assessments and feedback so that you create evidence that demonstrates these competencies. Keep track of these experiences so that you have a story to tell about your development of a competency.

- Based on your Roadmap, consider what experiences in student organizations, pro bono work, paid and unpaid clerkships, externships, and so on will best help you implement your Roadmap. Secure at least two such experiences that you will complete during your 2L year.

- Research test dates and decide when you want to take your state's ethics exam (if applicable). Many students take a Professional

Responsibility course during their 2L year. Consider whether you want to take the test soon after finishing the course, and plan accordingly.

b. September

- Meet with your career services professionals and a faculty member to review and get input on your application materials such as resume, cover letter, and writing sample.
- Schedule a mock interview.
- Create a one-minute elevator speech to make your value proposition.
- Create a list of the main points you will make and how you will make them so that an employer understands your value proposition and your experience in specific competencies in a 20-minute screening interview.

> ## Key Transition Point: Completion of OCI
>
> If you participated in your school's OCI process, after its completion you should reflect upon and update your Roadmap. What went well? What did you learn? Consider meeting with your coach or career services personnel to discuss future plans.

c. October

- Revisit your draft of the Roadmap and debrief with a coach.
- If possible, share the Roadmap with other trusted advisors and coaches and get feedback.
- Continue implementing your plan to build a tent of professional relationships and your Roadmap.

d. November

- Look carefully at the bar examination subjects in the state where you intend to take the bar. *Note that an increasing number of states are moving to the Uniform Bar Examination. Decide whether you want to take a course on each bar subject.*
- Before registration for the spring semester, plan out the sequence of courses for your last three semesters, including prerequisites. Consider if you want to take externships or clinic classes.

e. December

- Secure two references from faculty who know your work well. Ask them to focus on the strongest competencies you want to emphasize.
- In bullet-point format, draft a reference letter covering the aspects that you hope the faculty member might emphasize that support the value proposition you are trying to make to potential employers. Ask the faculty member if he or she would like to see this. This helps you to see how your persuasive case fits together.
- Continue implementing your plan to build a tent of professional relationships and your Roadmap.
- Update your resume to reflect first-semester grades, GPA, awards, experiences with competencies, and class rankings.
- Update your writing sample.

5. **2L Spring Semester**

   a. January

   - Check in with your school's office of career and professional development. Update them on your professional goals, if they have changed. If you are considering an appellate judicial clerkship after graduation, check for the application due date.
   - Revisit your Roadmap. With the help of your mentors and coaches, make any revisions or updates you feel are necessary.
   - Seek out opportunities in the curriculum to develop portfolios of experiences of the competencies you want to emphasize. Ask professors for assessments and feedback in order to create evidence that demonstrates these competencies.

> ## Key Transition Point: After Fall Grades
>
> You are halfway through law school! This is a great time to reflect on what went well and what can be adjusted in the future. Did you have any work or other experiences in the fall that confirmed or eliminated one of your top employment options? Did you grow to a later stage on any competency? Can you provide evidence of this growth? Meet with your coach or career services personnel to discuss the semester and get tips moving forward.

- Continue implementing your plan to build a tent of professional relationships. Set benchmarks or milestones for how many new contacts you will make each semester to implement your plan.
- Continue implementing your Roadmap.
- Apply for summer positions and routinely check job search engines for new opportunities.

b. February

- Begin searching for potential summer experiences and employment.
- Update your resume with any experiences you gained since the first semester.
- Continue implementing your networking plan and your Roadmap.
- Apply for summer positions.

Key Transition Point: Selecting 3L Courses

Before registration reflect upon and update your Roadmap. Be sure to include classes that support your value proposition.

c. March

- Apply for summer positions.
- Continue implementing your networking plan and your Roadmap.

d. April

- Continue implementing your networking plan and your Roadmap.

e. May

- Update your resume to reflect second-semester grades, GPA, awards, experiences in the competencies you are trying to emphasize, and class rankings.
- Update your writing sample.

Key Transition Point: After Spring Grades

This is a great time to reflect on what went well and what can be adjusted in the future. Did you have any work or other experiences in the fall that confirmed or eliminated one of your top employment options? Did you grow to a later stage on any competency? Can you provide evidence of this growth? Meet with your coach or career services personnel to discuss the semester and get tips moving forward.

- Continue implementing your plan to build a tent of professional relationships and your Roadmap.

6. **2L–3L Summer**

- Research and seek out employment, volunteer, and research opportunities for the summer that will help you both explore your most promising employment options and develop the competencies that you want to focus on.
- Reach out to attorneys in areas of law that interest you to schedule informational interviews. Implement your networking plan in general.
- If you have begun your summer work, remember that you need, at the minimum, one supervisor who really knows your work and strongest competencies.
- Continue researching and familiarizing yourself with legal employers in the geographic region and general field in which you want to work. Consider getting lists of alumni from your undergraduate institution and alumni from your law school who are lawyers in that region and field.
- Update your resume.
- Review your law school's job bank for fall experience opportunities.

> **Key Transition Point: Reflect on Summer Experience**
>
> Which of your top employment options have you confirmed or eliminated? Did you grow to a later developmental stage on any competency? What evidence do you have regarding growth to a later stage of your strongest competency?

7. **3L Year**

- Revisit your Roadmap with the help of mentors and coaches. Make any revisions or updates you feel are necessary.
- Continue implementing your plan to build a tent of professional relationships.
- Seek out opportunities in the curriculum to develop portfolios of experiences in the competencies you wish to embrace. Ask professors for assessment and feedback so that you acquire evidence that

demonstrates these competencies. Keep track of these experiences so that you have a story to tell about your development of a specific competency.

- Apply for the bar examination in the state where you plan to practice.
- Schedule a meeting with a representative from your school's office of career and professional development to talk about your post-graduation plans.
- Research and plan your bar examination preparation.
- Check online resources for post-graduation job postings.
- Apply for post-graduation jobs that interest you.
- Consider if you want to pursue trial court judicial clerkships. Trial court judges often begin accepting applications for post-graduate clerkships during spring semester of the 3L year.

Key Transition Point: After Fall Grades

This is a great time to reflect on what went well and what can be adjusted in the future. Did you have any work or other experiences in the fall that confirmed or eliminated one of your top employment options? Did you grow to a later stage on any competency? Can you provide evidence of this growth? Meet with your coach or career services personnel to discuss the semester and get tips moving forward.

CHAPTER 4

BUILDING A TENT OF RELATIONSHIPS WITH PROFESSIONALS WHO BOTH SUPPORT YOU AND TRUST YOU TO DO THE WORK OF A LAWYER

The ultimate goal of this Roadmap process is for you to gain a breadth of experiences doing the work of a lawyer during your remaining time in law school so that you can

1. thoughtfully discern your passion, motivating interests, and strengths that best fit with a geographic community of practice, a practice area and type of client, and type of employer;
2. develop your strengths to the next level; and
3. have evidence of your strengths that employers value.

To reach your professional goals, with respect to this next summer and your 2L year and in the long term, you need to build a tent of relationships with professionals who both support you and trust you to do the work of a lawyer. You have limited time and energy for professional-relationship building while you are in law school, so this chapter emphasizes the most effective relationship-building steps at each stage of your development. The chapter presents a progression of steps that may be useful to you, but you can do them in whatever order makes the most sense to you.

The next section discusses why a tent of relationships with professionals who both support you and trust you to do the work of a lawyer is foundational for your success. Section 2 then analyzes specific effective steps to use your limited time and energy to build your tent. Section 3 looks at barriers that may inhibit your professional-relationship tent-building.

1. Why a Tent of Relationships with Professionals Who Both Support You and Trust You to Do the Work of a Lawyer Is Foundational for Your Success

All effective and successful lawyers regardless of practice area have built and are continuing to build a tent of relationships with professionals who both support them and trust them to do the work. In the early years of practice, you need professional relationships with experienced lawyers and clients who trust you enough to give you work. In addition, in your work as an advocate for your client, your professional relationships that create trust with decision-makers and adversaries greatly benefit your client. In the words of Katherian Roe, chief federal public defender for the District of Minnesota,

> In law school, I disliked networking because I am an introvert, and I thought those other people are not like me and we have nothing in common. This was a serious misunderstanding on my part. After I started practicing criminal defense, I realized that in order to achieve good results for my clients and to create the changes I hoped for in the law, I had to have a wide network of people who knew me and trusted my work. I had to become a seed planter in as wide a circle of people as I could. It is not easy, but it is absolutely necessary.[25]

---

[25] Katherian Roe, Dist. of Minn. Chief Fed. Pub. Defender, at a University of St. Thomas Law Employment Advisory Committee Meeting (May 17, 2013).

In addition, the authors of a 2016 empirical study of the factors that influence the promotion to partner in a big law firm found that those factors include being able to create strong professional relationships. According to the book *Accelerating Lawyer Success: How to Make Partner, Stay Healthy, and Flourish in the Law Firm,*

> We found that lawyers who make partner within 10 years tend to have certain characteristics in common. For starters, they are highly networked within their firms. They are not just connected personally to their colleagues; they also know how to use others' expertise. In other words, partners don't just know people. They know who knows what, and are able to strategically leverage that information to get their work done effectively and efficiently. Beyond having a strong sense of where expertise lies in the firm, partners tend to develop more effective informal mentoring relationships than those who do not make partner.[26]

Lawyers who make partner are more likely to report having multiple informal mentors who played a role in their career development; 57 percent of lawyers who made partner reported having three or more informal mentors who influenced their careers, compared to only 26 percent who did not make partner. In other words, having one mentor is simply not sufficient to excel. Having multiple mentors will boost your chances of getting that brass ring.[27]

And remember—it is not enough to merely have informal mentors; it is up to you to be proactive and develop those relationships so that you get as much out of them as possible. Your mentors won't know what you need until you ask them; so, ask![28]

So, if you want to make partner, spend time working on your interpersonal skills. Most important, never forget how crucial relationships are to success.[29]

Whenever you are with practicing lawyers or judges, ask them about the importance of relationship building in their professional life. Ask what was most effective for them to build professional relationships when they were in law school and early in their career.

---

[26] Lori Berman, Heather Bock & Juliet Aiken, Accelerating Lawyer Success 7 (2016).

[27] *Id.* at 10.

[28] *Id.*

[29] *Id.*

2. The Most Effective Use of Your Limited Time and Energy to Build Your Tent

Chapter 1 explained that the required curriculum in law schools emphasizes the technical capacities and skills in Table 1 and that law students must proactively seek professional experiences to test "fit," to develop the Table 1 and Table 2 capacities and skills for doing the actual work of a lawyer, and to have evidence that they can do the work of a lawyer. In this process of seeking and doing these experiences that mimic the actual work of a lawyer, you will build a tent of relationships with professionals who support you and trust you to do the work.

What does it mean for an experienced lawyer or professor to trust that you can do the work of a lawyer? This means that the experienced lawyer/professor is seeing enough of your work for an informed professional judgment about

1. your Table 1 capacities and skills, particularly your legal research, legal analysis, and written and oral communication skills; and
2. your Table 2 capacities and skills, particularly your strong work ethic, your conscientiousness and attention to detail, your project management skills, and your teamwork and collaboration skills.

You can see that typically your 1L required course doctrinal professors in large sections at the end of the semester will have an informed professional judgment about your knowledge of the doctrinal law in the subject area, your legal analysis, and your written and oral communication skills. Your lawyering skills professor will in addition have an informed judgment about your research skills. In smaller sections, a professor may have seen enough work to have an informed professional judgment about other Table 1 and Table 2 capacities and skills.

Experienced lawyers/professors working on projects with a new entrant particularly want high-quality research, analysis, and writing delivered with total reliability and on time; good teamwork; attention to detail; and quick learning from mistakes. You are looking for opportunities with experienced lawyers and professors to demonstrate these capacities and skills that lead them to trust you to do the work. They will then have sufficient evidence of your strengths to provide a strong recommendation.

In the author's experience, the big law and elite government and judicial clerkship employers require high grades in the 1L required courses. All the other employers want to see grades high enough to predict strong probabilities of bar passage. Grades are a predictor that you have some of the needed capacities and skills to do the work of a lawyer. Once you are actually doing the work of new entrants on projects with experienced lawyers and professors and they observe your work, they are able to move beyond a prediction and say that you are good at the full range of needed capacities and skills.

Remember in all seven of the following steps to building a tent of professional relationships that you want to "lean" your tent-building efforts in any time period to help you with experiences that will give you insight into your fit with highest-priority geographic area, area of practice/type of client, and type of employer. Then after significant experiences, you reflect, and if you change your top priorities, you change your "lean" on your tent-building efforts.

a. Initial Steps in Building Your Tent of Professional Relationships

Step 1—Establish a relationship with one of your career services office professionals.

Ask them to review your Roadmap template, your resume, and your cover letter to your target potential employers and to help you line up a good summer experience between your 1L and 2L years if you have not yet secured it. Ask for a mock interview.

Step 2—If your grades in any required course indicate a risk of bar pass problems, establish a relationship with your academic support professionals.

Your school's academic support professionals will be enormously helpful in advising you on whether you are at some risk with respect to bar passage and helping you create and implement a written professional development plan to ensure that you will pass the bar.

Figure 3 shows Steps 1 and 2.

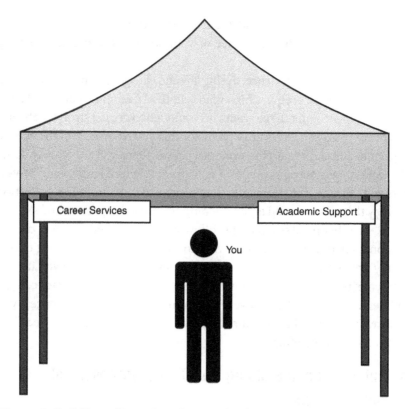

Figure 3 Building a Tent of Professional Relationships: Initial Steps

b. The Next Tent-Building Steps in the 1L Year

Step 3—If you don't have a good summer experience lined up yet, focus on relationships that will lead to a good summer experience.

If you don't yet have good paid or unpaid summer experience between your 1L and 2L years lined up the following sub-steps will help you achieve this goal.

    a.   Your school's career services professionals will have suggestions to help you.

    b.   See Chapter 3's timeline with suggestions and deadlines for some types of summer experience.

    c.   The Holloran Center has available online resources at the link in the footnote.[30]

---

[30] *Resources*, St. Thomas Sch. of L., https://law.stthomas.edu/about/centers-institutes /holloran-center/research-training/employment-roadmap/index.html (scroll down to "Third Edition Supplemental Materials"; link in bar at left) (last visited June 12, 2023).

d. You have a natural network of relationships with experienced lawyers and judges who will help you to find a good summer experience, including giving you a 20-minute informational interview.[31] Nathan Perez and Marcia Ballinger in *The 20-Minute Networking Meeting* (2016) conclude that approximately 70 percent of all jobs are obtained by candidates who come to an employer's attention through employee recommendations, referrals from trusted associates, or direct contact with a candidate who may be interviewing for a job. They recommend seeking 20-minute informational meetings to create brief, meaningful professional relationships that will lead to new information about your field, new contacts, and possibly more proactive steps to help you. The 20-minute informational meeting consists of a great first impression, a brief overview of your value proposition, a good discussion of your questions, and a strong ending. The Holloran Center has a short summary of these elements at the link in the footnote.[32]

The following list includes your natural network of lawyers who would respond to your request for an informational meeting.

i. Alumni of your law school in the geographic and practice areas that are your top Roadmap priorities. Your law school should have a lawyer search function on its website. LinkedIn also has a function where you can search for alumni of your school in a specified geographic and practice area. The Holloran Center has a short summary on how to use this LinkedIn function at the link in the footnote.[33] Note that while you can find these alumni on LinkedIn, it is more effective to use email to contact them.

ii. Lawyer alumni of your undergraduate school in the geographic and practice areas that are your top Roadmap

---

[31] I am grateful for suggestions on this concept of natural networks from Susan Fines, Monica Gould, and Robin Thorner.

[32] *Framework for 20-Minute Informational Interviews*, St. Thomas Sch. of L., https://law .stthomas.edu/about/centers-institutes/holloran-center/research-training/employment-road map/index.html (scroll down to "Third Edition Supplemental Materials"; link in bar at left) (last visited June 12, 2023).

[33] *Steps for LinkedIn Searches*, St. Thomas Sch. of L., https://law.stthomas.edu/about /centers-institutes/holloran-center/research-training/employment-roadmap/index.html (scroll down to "Third Edition Supplemental Materials"; link in bar at left) (last visited June 12, 2023).

priorities. The alumni office of your alma mater may help you. A LinkedIn search may also work to identify these lawyers.

iii. Connections to lawyers through your family and friend groups (e.g., who represented them?), your previous work experiences, or your social/athletic/community/church/volunteer/political groups.

iv. Upper-class students in your student organizations. Ask them for suggestions on what worked best for them at your stage.

v. Speakers at the law school including your student organizations. Introduce yourself. Follow up.

vi. Your professors. Ask if they need summer help on a project.

vii. Library and other staff at the law school beyond career services staff.

e. If summer experience that pays is not available, consider volunteering with organizations that appeal to you and offer your part-time help pro bono. The bar associations in the geographic area where you will spend the summer will have a list of pro bono opportunities for lawyers. Note that you could combine summer courses with volunteer work to get experience. In addition, smaller firms/employers may find your offer to work part-time more attractive to them, and you can combine paid and unpaid part-time experiences during the summer.

Step 4—Build professional relationships with professors—both full-time and adjunct.

In the 1L year, make a focused effort to get to know one professor outside of class reasonably well so the professor has some evidence of your Table 2 strengths. In the 2L year, take a seminar or supervised research involving a significant project and multiple drafts working with a professor. Focus on the capacities and skills mentioned earlier in section 2. Your goal by the end of the 2L year is that at least two professors have worked with you sufficiently on projects to trust that you can do the work of a lawyer and have evidence of your strengths. Keep a list of the projects you have done for a professor so that when you ask for a reference, you can remind the professor what you have done. Note that when you are asking for a reference, be sure to tell your professor what strengths you are emphasizing to potential employers.

Figure 4 shows Steps 1–4.

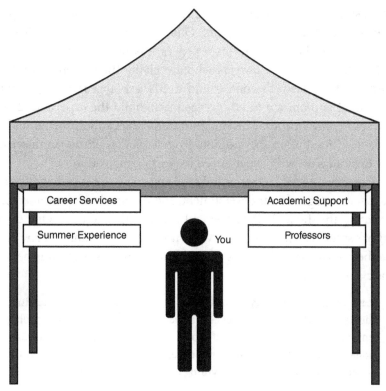

Figure 4 Building a Tent of Professional Relationships: Steps 1–4

c. Continuing Tent-Building Steps in the 2L and 3L Years

Step 5—Build professional relationships with practicing lawyers and judges.

Table 6 in Chapter 1 makes clear that legal employment and recommendations from practitioners or judges are the top two most helpful criteria for employers hiring students for post-graduation employment. The ideal goal here is that by the end of the summer between the 2L and 3L years, at least two practicing lawyers or judges have seen enough of your work on projects to trust that you can do the work of a lawyer and will provide a strong recommendation showing evidence of your strengths.

The author teaches a required Professional Responsibility fall semester course to 2L students. The first assignment is a short essay analyzing the most important "lessons learned" from the students' summer experience between the 1L and 2L years. One of the most important "lessons learned" from their summer experiences was how to interact productively with experienced lawyers who are giving the student work (e.g., understand the lawyer's context and needs, ask appropriate questions, check in at appropriate times, get feedback, build the experienced lawyer's confidence in you). The Holloran Center has a short memorandum available at the link in the footnote from a 2022 graduate summarizing how to build trust with experienced lawyers giving you work.[34]

The experienced lawyer or judge giving you work is essentially your client at this stage of your development, and you are developing and demonstrating the Table 2 capacities and skills in this context. One of the author's students who has built a very successful entertainment law practice (before law school he was a band leader, and his passion is helping musicians) emphasizes,

> It is not about you. It is about them; we are passionate about helping clients [including the experienced lawyer giving you work] solve problems and not just technical legal problems. They can feel if you are passionate about helping them. Over time, work to find your passion in helping them. Build trust. Everything else will take care of itself.[35]

You can ask an experienced lawyer or judge who has seen your work for a reference. Keep a list of the projects you have done for them so that when you ask for a reference, you can remind them what you have done. Also remember that when you are asking for a reference, be sure to tell them what strengths you are emphasizing to potential employers. You can also ask them to review your Roadmap plan and give you feedback.

Step 6—Build relationships with mentors and coaches.
Ida Abbott, a leading scholar on mentoring in the legal profession, has defined mentoring to be "a relationship-based process that helps individuals learn, grow and achieve high levels of professional success and

---

[34] *Building Relationships with Experienced Lawyers*, St. Thomas Sch. of L., https://law.stthomas.edu/about/centers-institutes/holloran-center/research-training/employment-road map/index.html (scroll down to "Third Edition Supplemental Materials"; link in bar at left) (last visited June 12, 2023).
[35] Comment from Ken Abdo to the author (May 3, 2017).

fulfillment."[36] Mentoring occurs when a more experienced and trusted lawyer takes an interest in a student's career development and success.[37] Mentors have relevant work and career experience, provide career and psychological support, and can create or directly affect career-enhancing opportunities.[38]

John Whitmore, author of the first book on workplace coaching,[39] defines coaching as "unlocking people's potential to increase their own performance. It is helping them to learn rather than teaching them."[40] Coaching helps people "to clarify their purpose and vision, achieve their goals, and reach their potential."[41] Whitmore believes mentoring is more about sharing expertise and passing down knowledge with some guidance.[42]

Mentoring emphasizes relationship-based career support for students by mentors with relevant work and career experience who use their own experience, insight, and advice to help mentees learn and progress. Coaching focuses on developing a student's self-understanding and discernment of purpose, vision and goals, and self-direction in terms of the creation and implementation of a plan to achieve them. Abbott points out that the lines between mentoring and coaching are fluid, since both roles "provide individualized and personal support by a trusted advisor."[43] She also notes that "as coaching becomes more popular, boundaries between mentoring and coaching will blur and overlap."[44]

You need mentors/coaches. Ideally you will proactively build a professional relationship with one or more mentors/coaches who have the skills in Table 8.[45]

---

[36] *Mentoring*, IDA ABBOTT CONSULTING, https://idaabbott.com/mentoring/ (last visited May 12, 2023).

[37] IDA O. ABBOTT, LAWYERS' PROFESSIONAL DEVELOPMENT 212 (2d ed. 2012).

[38] IDA ABBOTT, THE LAWYER'S GUIDE TO MENTORING 42–43 (2d ed. 2018).

[39] JOHN WHITMORE, COACHING FOR PERFORMANCE 1 (5th ed. 2017).

[40] *Id.* at 248.

[41] *Id.*

[42] *Id.* at 14, 249.

[43] ABBOTT, *supra* note 14, at 41.

[44] *Id.* at 38.

[45] This table was first published in Neil Hamilton, *Mentor/Coach: The Most Effective Curriculum to Foster Each Student's Professional Development and Formation*, 17 UNIV. ST. THOMAS L.J. 836, 855 (2022).

Table 8 Foundational Competencies for a Law Student's Mentor/Coach

---

1. Actively listening to understand the student's developmental stage and goals

2. Asking powerful, open questions to foster the student's guided reflection and self-assessment and raise the student's awareness and responsibility

3. Facilitating student growth toward later stages of the Table 1 and Table 2 capacities and skills by transforming learning and insight (especially from professional experiences doing the work of a lawyer) into clear and realistic goals, options, and action[46]

4. Understanding and respecting the student's context and identity and providing support, empathy, and concern for the student

---

You can see how valuable a mentor/coach with the capacities and skills in Table 8 will be for your professional development. Recall the empirical findings in section 1 of this chapter about the importance of mentors to lawyers who made partner in a big firm.

Recruiting a mentor/coach to help you is an art form where you improve with practice. If your school has a formal program to match you with a mentor, try the program. The challenge is that formal mentor-matching programs may or may not lead to a mentor/coach for you with the skills in Table 8. In addition, in order for an experienced lawyer/judge to invest in you as your mentor/coach, there has to be some "chemistry" between you. This type of relationship takes some time to grow. Here are some ideas to help you be proactive in recruiting mentors/coaches.

You may already have a mentor/coach in your professional network. It may be an experienced lawyer or judge for whom you have been work-ing. If you have done some work for them that they have appreciated and valued, then you have a start on building a mentor/coach relationship. Be proactive. Make the effort to grow that relationship into an ongoing and continuing one. You can add value to their life. For example, read blogs/articles both in their practice area and on the future of legal work and the profession. They want to know about these topics and about your generation's views on them. Holloran Center at the link in the foot-note has available a memorandum with links to the best blogs.[47] Show

---

[46] WHITMORE, *supra* note 15, at 254.

[47] *Best Blogs*, ST. THOMAS SCH. OF L., https://law.stthomas.edu/about/centers-institutes /holloran-center/research-training/employment-roadmap/index.html (scroll down to "Third Edition Supplemental Materials"; link in bar at left) (last visited June 12, 2023).

appreciation and gratitude. The author's experience is that it is extremely rewarding if a student/early career lawyer for whom I am a mentor/coach sends me notes when they achieve some new step in their professional development.

You can ask experienced lawyers or judges for whom you have worked how they found mentors and coaches. You can ask them who are the lawyers or judges they most admire and whether they would make an introduction for you to meet them. A mentor/coach relationship grows organically over time, so generally, don't ask directly, "Will you be my mentor/coach?"

Step 7—Expand your tent of professional relationships.
In any time period, stay focused on building your tent of professional relationships in your current highest-priority areas of practice, type of client, and type of employer. A particularly effective way to develop your relationships with practicing lawyers and judges in those areas is to find out what type of pro bono/volunteer work they do. Join in contributing to the work.

You can join the bar association section in your areas of highest interest and attend events and CLEs. Attend student organization or law school events where practicing lawyers/judges are speaking. Focus on having a meaningful conversation with one or two experienced lawyers who will remember your name. Follow up. If you are reading blogs/articles about the practice area as discussed earlier, you have topics to talk to them about that they will find interesting. You can offer to help the executive committee of the relevant bar section with a project.

Note the importance of your cross-cultural skills in this type of outreach. Be intentional about building professional relationships that develop these skills. You can assess your stage of development on cross-cultural relationship skills and read some suggestions on how to build these skills at the link in the footnote.[48]

Figure 5 shows Steps 1–7.

---

[48] *Developing Cross Cultural Competency*, ST. THOMAS SCH. OF L., https://law.stthomas .edu/about/centers-institutes/holloran-center/research-training/employment-roadmap/index .html (scroll down to "Third Edition Supplemental Materials"; link in bar at left) (last visited June 12, 2023).

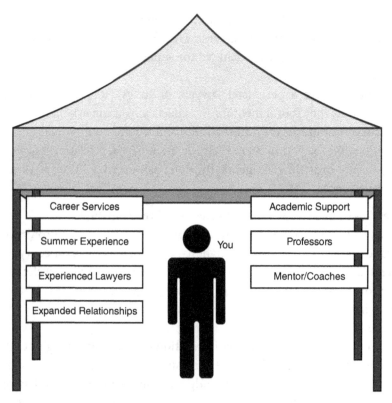

Figure 5 Building a Tent of Professional Relationships: Steps 1–7

3. Barriers That May Inhibit Your Professional Relationship Tent-Building

This section looks at common barriers that may inhibit your professional relationship tent-building. These barriers are surmountable. You are completely capable of building an effective tent.

a. You Struggle with Lack of Time and Energy

Many students struggle to find time to build professional relationships since the time demands of law school courses are substantial. In addition, those courses do not require professional relationship tent-building, so how important could this activity be? Keep in mind, as Chapter 1 discussed, that for historical reasons the required curriculum in legal education has put too much emphasis on doctrinal law knowledge and legal analysis. Conversely, and more effectively, medical education requires professional relationship tent-building in the experiential rotations in the third and fourth year.

Ask experienced lawyers in the practice areas of most interest to you about the importance of building their tent of relationships with professionals who trust them to do the work and support them. Ask them how they find time and energy to do it. What strategies have been most effective for them?

In your case as a student, your goals are to (1) gain experience so that you can discern how your passion, motivating interests, and strengths best fit with a geographic area, practice area and type of client, and type of employer; (2) develop your strengths to the next level; and (3) have evidence of your strengths that employers value. The author suggests both staying focused on these three goals in any semester and setting a specific goal of two hours a week for this effort; calendar the time on your schedule each week. At the end of each semester, review whether you have reached your goals for building a tent of professional relationships for that semester. Reflect on your evaluation and revise your plan.

b. You May Think Professional-Relationship Building Is Fundamentally Instrumental and Manipulative in Nature

You are entering a service profession where professional relationships built on trust in you are foundational. Think of the dentist, electrician, or plumber to whom your family and you turn for help. These business relationships are built on trust that the service provider cares about helping your family at a reasonable cost and are not fundamentally instrumental or manipulative in nature.

Dr. Ivan Misner defines professional-relationship building as more about farming than it is about hunting. Remember Federal Public Defender Katherian Roe's observation in section 1 of this chapter: "I had to become a seed planter in as wide a circle of people as I could." It is about cultivating trust relationships with other professionals and clients and taking the time and energy to help them grow and flourish.[49] Farming and seed planting are not instrumental and manipulative.

---

[49] Ivan Misner, *Networking—The TRUE Definition* (May 9, 2022), https://ivanmisner.com /networking-the-true-definition.

c. You Have Nothing to Offer and Don't Know What to Say

You may feel that you have nothing to offer to experienced lawyers and judges with whom you hope to develop a professional relationship. It is important to remember that many experienced lawyers and judges have an intrinsic desire to "pay forward" the help that they received earlier from experienced lawyers and to help the profession. It means a great deal to them to make a positive difference in a new lawyer's life, especially if the new lawyer expresses gratitude for the help. It is an honor to be asked to use your experience to help a new lawyer. Experienced lawyers and judges are living within the social contract that Albert Einstein observed:

> A hundred times a day I remind myself that my inner and outer life depends on the labors of others, living and dead, and that I must exert myself in order to give in the same measure as I have received and am still receiving.[50]

They hope that as you gain experience, you will also give back.

Experienced lawyers and judges are also very interested in what the newer generations of law students and lawyers think about the opportunities and challenges for our profession. Spend 15 to 20 minutes a week reading some of the most influential blogs (discussed earlier) in the areas of law that interest you and ask experienced lawyers and judges to whom you are reaching out what they think on current "hot topics" in the field.

d. You Experience Imposter Phenomenon

Psychologists Pauline Rose Clance and Suzanne Imes defined imposter phenomenon as "an internal experience of intellectual phoniness . . . despite outstanding academic and professional accomplishments."[51] Professor David Grenardo explains, "Imposter syndrome creates a fear in an individual that they do not belong, and others who do belong will soon discover they are a fraud."[52] "People who suffer from imposter syndrome

---

[50] ALBERT EINSTEIN, THE EXPANDED QUOTABLE EINSTEIN 11 (Alice Calaprice ed., 2000).

[51] Pauline Rose Clance & Suzanne Imes, *The Imposter Phenomenon in High Achieving Adult Women: Dynamics and Therapeutic Intervention*, 15 PSYCHOTHERAPY: THEORY, RSCH. & PRAC. 241 (1978).

[52] David A. Grenardo, *The Phantom Menace to Professional Identity Formation and Law Success: Imposter Syndrome*, 47 U. DAYTON L. REV. 369, 370–71 (2022) (citing Diana Uchiyama, *Imposter Syndrome: Do You Feel Like a Fraud?*, 108 ILL. BAR J. 52 (2020)).

attribute their success to luck, good timing, or other external factors as opposed to their own abilities, intelligence, and hard work. . . . They feel unworthy of a position or promotion because they doubt their competence or expertise."[53]

Every new entrant to the professions, whether a law student or a medical student, has to deal with the initial reality that they lack experience and essentially must answer a difficult question: "How do I build confidence and overcome my self-doubt when I don't know what I am doing?" Even veteran lawyers face totally new situations with substantial complexity where they may feel "I don't know what I am doing," but they have confidence in their basic problem-solving skills and know that, with the help of others if needed, "I will figure this out." A veteran in-house counsel was asked to remark on the confidence issue inherent in judgment calls while practicing. The lawyer responded,

> The more experienced you get, the more comfortable you become in telling yourself that you are really just cobbling together this whole thing. Your facts are changing, the clock is ticking, and you have to give an answer. It's your best call in that situation. And sometimes, you feel that you have no idea. But you do. You have an idea, and you have to offer your best one.[54]

The author's experience is similar. It is always best judgment, given the time and resources available. And it doesn't change for senior lawyers. We have the experience of professionally masking our uncertainty and nervousness, but we are still just giving our best judgment in complex problems where there is some significant degree of uncertainty.

Hopefully, you are noticing that developing this confidence and good judgment is a process and a journey, not simply a checkmark in your skills portfolio. You are learning to "fake it till you make it," so to speak. But "making it" is different from what you may have thought earlier. It is not certainty; it is a growing sense of confidence that under conditions of substantial uncertainty working with others including the client, "I can figure out reasonable solutions." This is a process of acculturation into a confidence that comes primarily through experiences with

---

[53] *Id.* at 372.

[54] Email from Andrew Pugh, Gen. Counsel, Children's Hosp. & Clinics of Minn., to author (July 7, 2015, 02:00 p.m. CST) (on file with author).

problem-solving. Through experiences and reflection, you will learn that you have the skills to solve problems competently, and you will in effect gain the requisite confidence. Your Roadmap template is about your plan to gain needed experience, and you will continue to reflect and revise your plan as you get experience.

Know that every lawyer before you has traveled this same developmental path and that you are developing the necessary capacities and skills to practice law. You will find as you enter practice that you are a good problem-solver and you are getting better. At the very least, you will be able to quickly identify important facts, frame an issue, and bring possible solutions to the table in a way that others will not. Furthermore, you are developing the capability of asking good questions, researching the law and potential solutions, and offering an answer according to your best judgment in the context of uncertainty. If the problem is complex, you simply must take your best initial shot at identifying the issues and possible solutions. Then find creative ways to ask for advice from experienced lawyers in your tent of those who support you.

CHAPTER 5

COMPLETING THE ONLINE TEMPLATE FOR BUILDING A TENT OF PROFESSIONAL RELATIONSHIPS

https://law.stthomas.edu/about/centers-institutes/holloran-center
/research-training/employment-roadmap/index.html
Please read Chapter 4 first. You may need to refer to Chapter 4 for longer
descriptions of some of the steps in this template.

This template focuses on building a tent of relationships with professionals who both support you and trust you to do the work of a lawyer.
Steps 1–4 emphasize specific professional relationships you should be
building in the 1L year. Step 5 involves professional relationships with
practicing lawyers and judges who have observed your work and trust
you to do the work of a lawyer. Step 6 asks you to build a professional
relationship with one or more mentors/coaches. Some 1L students may
already have these Step 5 and Step 6 professional relationships, but many
students will be building them in the summers between the 1L and 2L
year and the 2L and 3L year, plus other experiences mimicking the actual
work of a lawyer during the 2L and 3L years. Step 7 addresses expanding

your tent of professional relationships beyond those covered in Steps 1–6. A student in any year of law school can be developing professional relationships with practicing lawyers and judges at law school or bar association events.

Remember that in any time period, you are "leaning" your professional-relationship tent-building efforts to help you with experiences that will test your fit with your answers to Step 5 of the Roadmap template regarding geographic area, area of practice/type of client, and type of employer.

Fill in the template with reasonably brief answers. You can use bullet points. Remember that a coach who will help you with feedback will have time to read only reasonably brief answers.

Building a Tent of Professional Relationships Template

Name of Student: _____

Step 1—Have you established a relationship with one of your school's career services professionals and asked them to review your resume, your cover letter, and your Roadmap template and give you feedback?

Yes _____

No _____

If "no," provide a specific date by which you will establish this relationship. _____

Step 2—Do your grades in any required course indicate a risk of bar pass problems? If you are uncertain, see your academic support staff at your law school.

Yes _____

No _____

If "yes," have you seen your academic support staff to create and implement a written professional development plan that will maximize probabilities of passing the bar?

Yes _____

No _____

If "no," provide a specific date by which you will establish this plan.

_____

Step 3—Do you have good summer experience lined up?

Yes _____

No _____

If "yes," where is the summer experience? _____

_____

If "no," this is a top priority for the time you have available before the middle of the spring semester, after which you will be increasingly focused on end-of-semester tasks. Read Chapter 4, Step 3, sub-steps a–e. Focus first on the suggestions of your law school's career services professional with whom you have a relationship. Then emphasize your natural network outlined in Chapter 4, Step 3, sub-step d. You are focused particularly on professional relationships that will help you test your fit with your answers to Step 5 of the Roadmap template. Twenty-minute informational meetings with lawyers and judges in your natural network will be useful. List five specific outreach actions you will take with your natural network to be completed by a specific date.

Outreach action 1: _____. By this date: _____.

Outreach action 2: _____. By this date: _____.

Outreach action 3: _____. By this date: _____.

Outreach action 4: _____. By this date: _____.

Outreach action 5: _____. By this date: _____.

Step 4—By the end of the 1L year, will you have a professional relationship with one professor who has good evidence of your Table 2 strengths that you identified in Step 3 of the Roadmap template?

Name of the professor: _____.

What evidence does the professor have of your Table 2 strengths?

_____

If you do not yet have this type of professional relationship with a professor, what outreach actions will you be taking to create such a relationship?

Name of the professor: _____.

Outreach action #1: _____. What is the date by which you will take this action?

_____

Outreach action #2: _____. What is the date by which you will take this action?

_____

Note that a goal by the end of the 2L year is to have two strong professional relationships of this type with professors.

Step 5—This step focuses on professional relationships with practicing lawyers and judges who have seen your work sufficiently to trust

that you can do the work of a lawyer (see Chapter 4 for a definition of the work of a lawyer in this context). For most 1L students, this is a major goal for the summer between the 1L and 2L years, and then for 2L students, this is also a major goal for the summer between the 2L and 3L years.

Some 1L students may already have a professional relationship with a practicing lawyer or judge who has seen a sufficient amount of the student's work to trust that the student can do the work of a lawyer. If you have such a relationship, put the lawyer or judge's name here: _____. Plus a short description of the work you have done for the lawyer or judge:

_____.

If you don't yet have such a relationship, then fill in this step at the end of the 1L–2L summer. Put the lawyer or judge's name here:

_____.

Plus a short description of the work you have done for the lawyer or judge:

_____.

Step 6—This step requires a professional relationship with a mentor/ coach defined in Step 6 of Chapter 4.

Do you already have a professional relationship with a mentor/coach who meets that definition?

Yes _____

No _____

If "yes," please put the lawyer or judge's name here along with their position: _____.

If "no," what outreach actions do you plan to take to create this type of relationship?

Outreach action #1: _____

_____. What is the date by which you will take this action?

_____

Outreach action #2: _____

_____. What is the date by which you will take this action?

_____

Step 7—This final step focuses on expanding your tent of professional relationships.

Read Chapter 4, Step 7.

What outreach action steps have you taken during this academic year to expand your tent of professional relationships?

Outreach action #1: _____.

Outreach action #2: _____.

What outreach actions do you intend to take during the remainder of this academic year to expand your tent of professional relationships?

Outreach action #1: _____

_____. What is the date by which you will take this action?

_____

Outreach action #2: _____

_____. What is the date by which you will take this action?

_____

Remember to have a file system to keep track of these professional relationships and to stay in touch with them.

If at all possible, ask an experienced lawyer or judge to give you feedback on this plan.